I0837690

**Dedicated to my Wife
and Son**

ANIMAL FACES
CARAS DE ANIMALES

LOVESTER
POSEY

ANTELOPE

ANTÍLOPE

BEAR

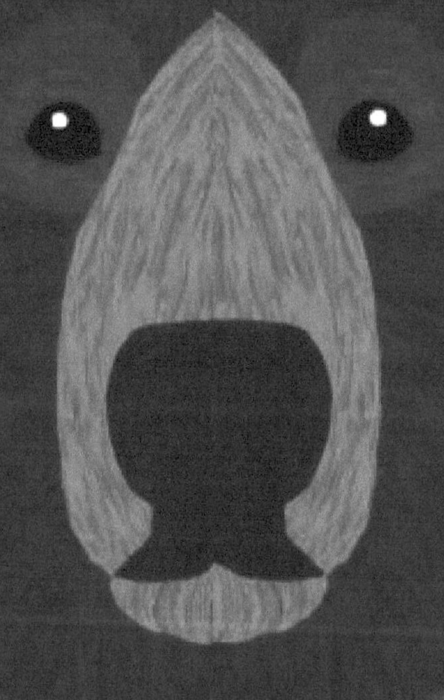

OSO

CARDINAL

CARDENAL

CAT

GATO

CHEETAH

GUEPARDO

COW 
VACA

DOG 
PERRO

FROG

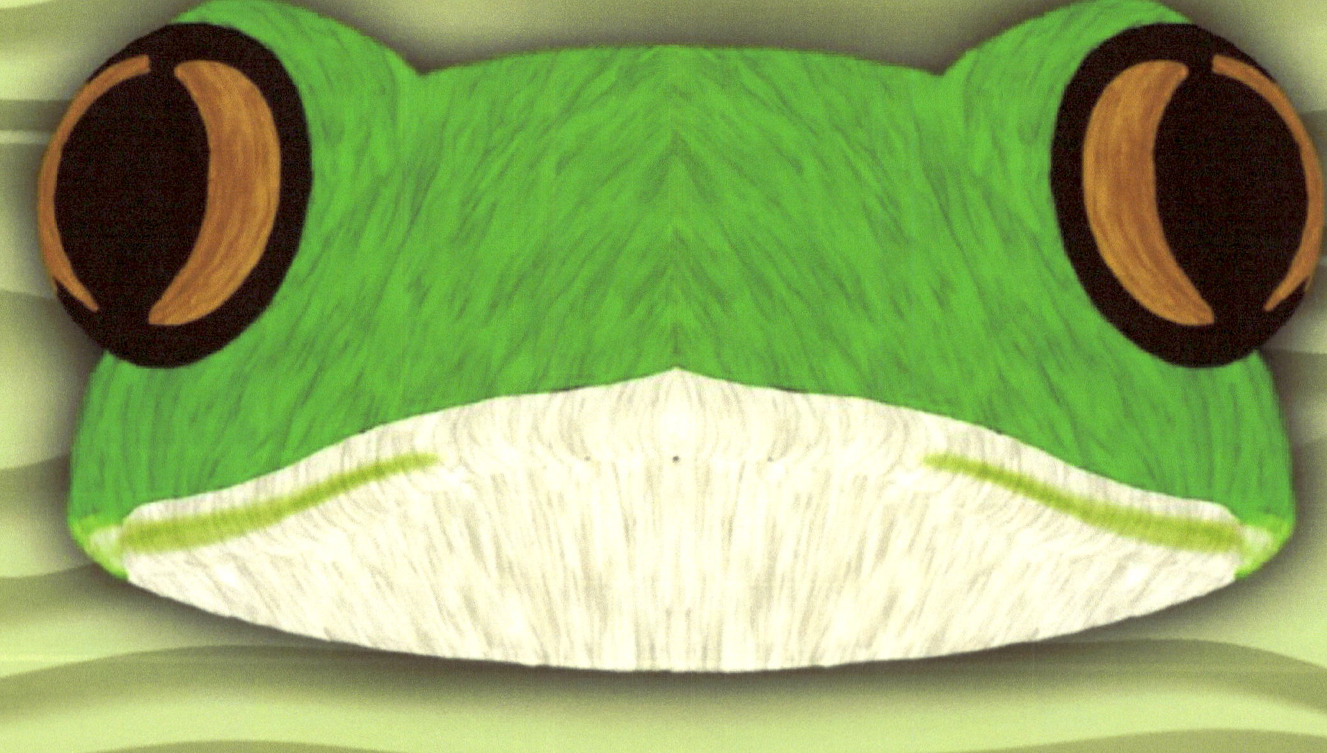

RANA

GIRAFFE
JIRAFA

KOALA

KOALA

MANDRILL

MANDRIL

OWL 
BÚHO

RACCOON
MAPACHE

SLOTH
PEREZOSO

TIGER
TIGRE

ZEBRA
CEBRA

COLORS

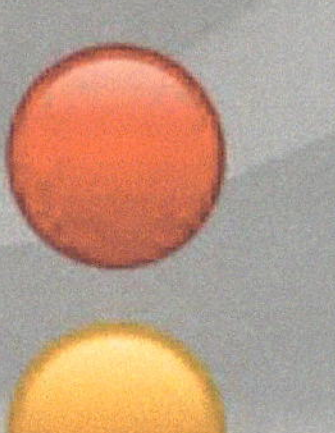

COLORES

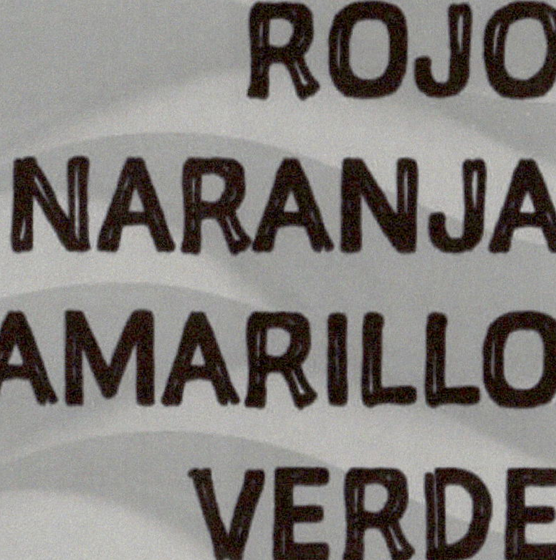

RED	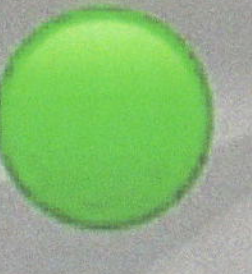	ROJO
ORANGE		NARANJA
YELLOW		AMARILLO
GREEN		VERDE
BLUE	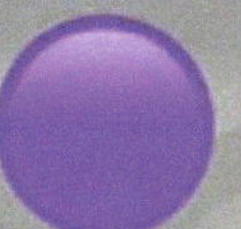	AZUL
VIOLET		MARADO
BLACK		NEGRO
WHITE	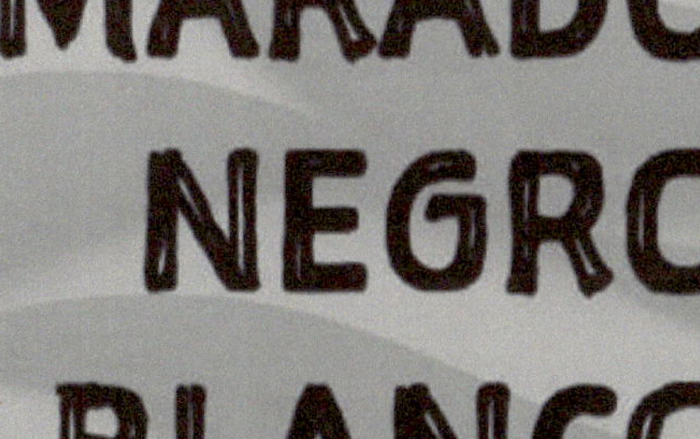	BLANCO

DAYS OF THE WEEK

DÍAS DE LA SEMANA

SUNDAY	DOMINGO
MONDAY	LUNES
TUESDAY	MARTES
WEDNESDAY	MIÉRCOLES
THURSDAY	JUEVES
FRIDAY	VIERNES
SATURDAY	SÁBADO

NUMBERS

NÚMEROS

ZERO	0	CERO
ONE	1	UNO
TWO	2	DOS
THREE	3	TRES
FOUR	4	CUATRO
FIVE	5	CINCO
SIX	6	SEIS
SEVEN	7	SIETE
EIGHT	8	OCHO
NINE	9	NUEVE
TEN	10	DIEZ